20TH CENTURY

fashion

THE 20S & 30S

FLAPPERS & VAMPS

For a free color catalog describing Gareth Stevens Publishing's list of high-quality books and multimedia programs, call 1-800-542-2595 (USA) or 1-800-461-9120 (Canada). Gareth Stevens Publishing's Fax: (414) 225-0377.

Library of Congress Cataloging-in-Publication Data available upon request from publisher. Fax: (414) 225-0377 for the attention of the Publishing Records Department.

ISBN 0-8368-2599-3

This North American edition first published in 2000 by
Gareth Stevens Publishing
1555 North RiverCenter Drive, Suite 201
Milwaukee, Wisconsin 53212 USA

Original edition © 1999 by David West Children's Books. First published in Great Britain in 1999 by Heinemann Library, Halley Court, Jordan Hill, Oxford OX2 8EJ, a division of Reed Educational and Professional Publishing Limited. This U.S. edition © 2000 by Gareth Stevens, Inc. Additional end matter © 2000 by Gareth Stevens, Inc.

Editor: Clare Oliver
Picture Research: Carlotta Cooper/Brooks Krikler Research
Consultant: Helen Reynolds

Gareth Stevens Series Editor: Dorothy L. Gibbs

Photo Credits:
Abbreviations: (t) top, (m) middle, (b) bottom, (l) left, (r) right

Corbis: pages 21(br), 23(br), 29(m)
Mary Evans Picture Library: Cover (tr, m), pages 3(tr), 4(t), 5(ml), 6(bl), 7(br), 8(tr, b), 11(tl, tr), 12(tl), 13(br), 14(bl), 15(tl), 16(b), 17(br), 18(tl, b) 19(tr, br), 22(mr), 24(bl)
Hulton Getty: pages 6(br), 8(tl), 9(t, b), 12-13(t), 14-15, 15(br), 18-19, 19(bl), 24-25, 25(tr), 26(tl), 29(tr, br)
Kobal Collection: Cover (tl, bl), pages 3(tl), 4(b), 8-9, 12-13(b), 22(tl), 22-23, 23(tr, l), 25(br)
© *Vogue*/Condé Nast Publications Ltd. / Beaton: Cover (mr, br), pages 3(br), 7(bl), 27(bl) / Bruehl-Bourges: pages 10(tl), 17(ml) / Helen Dryden: page 10(b) / Carl Erickson: page 26(br) / Hoyningen-Huene: page 17(tr) / Georges Lepape: pages 16(tl) / H. Meserdle: Cover (ml), page 6(t) / George W. Plank: page 11(br) / Douglas Pollard: page 13(mr) / Schenker: pages 27(tr), 28 / Scotts: page 24 (tl) / Steichen: pages 7(t), 11(bl) / Studio Sun: page 5(br) / *Vogue* Magazine: Cover (bm), pages 5(t), 10(tr), 12(bl), 14(t), 15(tr), 16(tr), 20(tl, tr, br), 21(tl, tr, bl), 26(m) / *Vogue* Studio: page 27(br)

With special thanks to the Picture Library and Syndication Department at *Vogue* Magazine/Condé Nast Publications Ltd.

Printed in Mexico

1 2 3 4 5 6 7 8 9 04 03 02 01 00

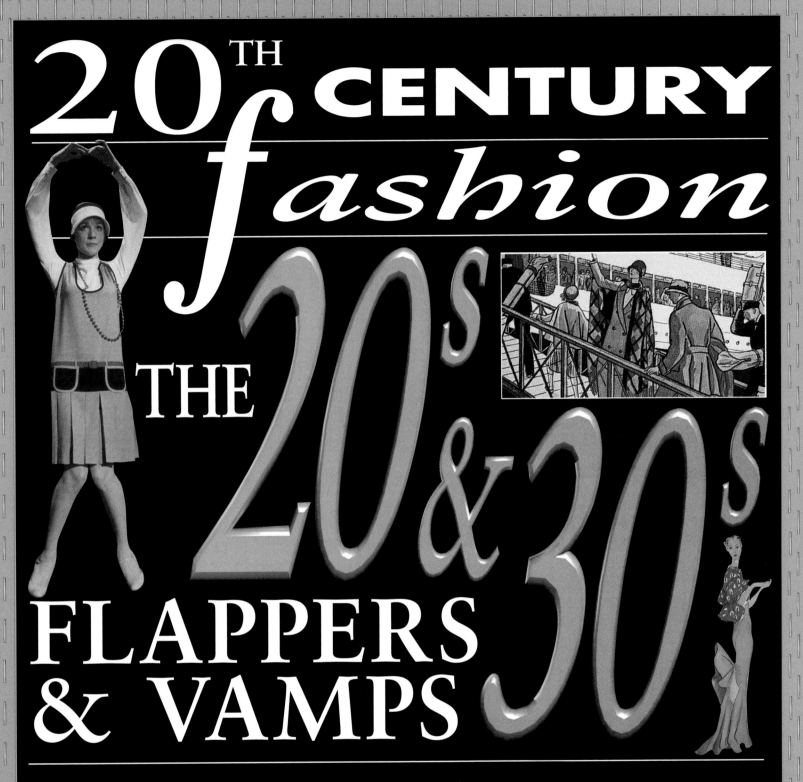

20TH CENTURY fashion

THE 20s & 30s

FLAPPERS & VAMPS

Cally Blackman

Gareth Stevens Publishing
MILWAUKEE

Contents

The 1920s saw some wild dance crazes, such as the Charleston, advertised here at the Folies-Bergère cabaret in Paris.

Gang warfare in the United States inspired a string of gangster films. The Public Enemy (1931) was one of many starring James Cagney.

Between the Wars

After the horrors of World War I, the early 1920s brought a general feeling of freedom. Women who had worked during the war found new financial and social independence. Vamps and flappers — boyish young women who wore makeup and skimpy dresses and smoked in public — dominated the social scene.

The gaiety, however, was short-lived. Many European countries had large war debts, which, along with rising inflation and stock market disasters, led to the worst economic recession of the 20th century. Europe was also in political turmoil. In Spain, fascism and communism fought a bloody civil war (1936–39) that inspired Spanish painter Pablo Picasso's masterpiece *Guernica* (1937). The United States introduced Prohibition, but, far from putting an end to alcohol, it created a black market controlled by gangsters. The most famous gangster, Al Capone, was said to be worth $100 million in 1927.

As always, fashion was influenced by the events around it. When the Depression took hold, wild flapper dresses gave way to sober but feminine fashions. Movies were the chief form of entertainment, and Hollywood led the styles. Macy's in New York, for example, sold 500,000 copies of an evening gown worn by Joan Crawford. When World War II broke out, in 1939, the silver screen would be the only source of glamour and escapism for several years to come.

In 1925, flappers wore drop-waisted dresses decorated with pearls, crystals, and tiny mirrors. Haircuts were short and boyish.

Shopping became a hobby, as happy shoppers traveled to the big department stores and came home laden with parcels. Even working in a department store was glamorous. Film star Greta Garbo was "discovered" as a shop girl in Stockholm!

By the 1930s, the chief item of daywear was the suit, and hemlines again dropped below the knee. Sensible styles reflected the economic worries of the time.

Girls Will Be Boys

During World War I, many women had worked for the first time. After the war, new financial independence and greater equality enabled women to pursue freer lifestyles. By 1928, all women over age twenty-one in Britain could vote. The sex barriers were gradually breaking down.

This Vogue *cover (1924) showed the fashion for costume jewelry. Beads were worn long and sometimes knotted.*

SIMPLY SHORT

Women's fashions reflected their new liberation, and, as women led more active lives, styles became more practical. Clothes were shaped like tubes with dropped waistlines, and skirts became shorter. A dress or a skirt and blouse was very fashionable worn under a long coat that had lining to match the dress. Wool or tweed suits, often belted at the waist, were also worn during the day. The wealthy sometimes wore them with fur collars.

FLATTER FIGURES

The emphasis was on youth and a slim, boyish body. Underwear became simpler. Corsets were replaced by cylindrical underwear that flattened the chest and had garters to hold up stockings. Some young people even went without petticoats!

Before 1924, stockings were made of dark wool or cotton. With the invention of rayon came "nude" stockings that showed off the legs.

COCO CHANEL

Probably the most influential designer of the 1920s, Coco Chanel's elegant clothes inspired the *garçonne* (French for *boy*) look. Her cardigan suits, sailor jackets, pullovers, and trousers were made of soft, jersey fabrics and were worn with costume jewelry. She was one of the first to open a boutique.

In 1921 Coco Chanel (shown below, in a cardigan suit) launched her Chanel No. 5 perfume. Five was her lucky number.

COLORS OF FASHION

Neutral colors, such as beige, were common. Beige was sometimes called "the ghost of khaki" because so much of that dye was left over after the war. The influence of the Russian Ballet, however, brought in brighter colors, such as purple and orange, particularly for evening wear.

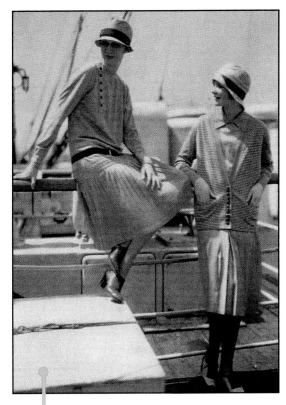

Hats were always worn outside during the day. The most fashionable hat was the cloche (French for bell*), as worn by this* Vogue *cover girl (1924).*

BOYISH BOBS

Women started to cut their hair during the war to avoid accidents in the factories. By the early 1920s, almost everyone was wearing the fashionable bob, and then the shingle, which was slightly waved. After these styles came the even more boyish Eton crop.

In 1926, Coco Chanel's easy-to-wear clothes included the drop-waisted jersey dress (left) and a silk skirt worn with a jersey sweater and a cardigan (right).

FABULOUS FOOTWEAR

Shoes had low, Cuban, or Louis (hourglass-shaped) heels with a strap across the instep. Evening shoes were often decorated with a buckle, much like the shoes worn by men in the 1700s. Russian boots were popular when skirts were at their shortest.

Sewing machines were cheap to buy, so many women made their own clothes, including the new, simpler underwear styles.

CHEAP CHIC

Affordable, ready-made fashions became available in stores, such as the Co-op, or Burton's for menswear. It was easy to follow fashion in the many new women's magazines that were produced. Home dress-making became popular, with magazines featuring patterns for sewing, knitting, and crocheting.

WELDON'S HOME DRESSMAKER N° 472

LADIES' UNDERWEAR

4D

FREE—ALL these Slim-Line PATTERNS

The Great Gatsby

In the 1920s, older men still wore Edwardian-style clothes — formal morning coats or frock coats, and tails and white ties for evening wear. Younger men, however, wore a more relaxed style.

Both males and females wore knickerbockers. In the U.S., a law had to be changed before women could wear them.

It was fashionable to spend the week in town and weekends in the country. Even on weekends, men wore double-breasted suits and panama hats.

LOUNGING AROUND

Lounge suits, made in soft fabrics, such as checked tweeds and gray flannel, were cut loosely for comfort. Shoulders were wider, armholes were bigger, jackets were longer, and trousers had more room at the top. Zippers began to replace buttoned flies. Soft shirt collars replaced stiff, starched ones for informal wear. Ties often had bright patterns, but, sometimes, were not worn at all. Patent leather shoes were popular with evening wear, but brogues were the style for daytime. While some men still wore two-tone spats, gradually, they were worn only for formal occasions.

Men had more fashion choices than ever before. These fashion plates show the formal, casual, and sporty looks worn around 1927.

Author F. Scott Fitzgerald was known for his own fast living. His 1925 novel The Great Gatsby *documents the wild excesses of the rich during the 1920s. In 1974, this story was made into a movie starring Robert Redford as Jay Gatsby.*

It was polite to wear a hat outdoors. Artist Cecil Beaton (left) attended the 1927 annual Eton-Harrow match in a "topper." For less formal occasions, boaters, Homburgs, and panama hats were popular styles.

BAGGY TROUSERS

In 1925, some fashionable young men at Oxford University started the rage for wearing Oxford bags, baggy flannel trousers that were 20 inches (0.5 meters) wide at the bottom — or more! Adapted from sportswear, these trousers were one of the most outrageous styles of the century.

OFF THE RACK

Those who could afford to went to a tailor for their suits. London tailoring was considered to be the best in the world. Although ready-made suits were becoming increasingly available, they tended not to fit very well.

THE DUKE OF WINDSOR

The Duke of Windsor (shown at right, in 1937) was a key fashion figure. He wore generously cut suits in colorful tweeds, checks, or stripes, and he introduced the "Windsor knot" for ties. He also started the trend for patterned Fair Isle sweaters in 1922.

The Duke of Windsor became, briefly, King Edward VIII of Britain, but he abdicated in 1936 to marry an American divorcée, Wallis Warfield Simpson (left).

Art Deco: A Total Look

Art deco was the most important design movement of the 1920s and the forerunner of modernism in the 1930s. It swept away the graceful and intricate lines of art nouveau.

The art deco style was seen mostly in interior design, but it influenced all other arts, from fashion to packaging.

DECORATIVE ARTS

Art deco design took its name from a Paris exhibition held in 1925, called the *Exposition Internationale des Arts Decoratifs et Industriels Modernes*. The style was influenced by major artistic movements, such as cubism and futurism, which celebrated the fast-moving modernization of the time. These art styles often featured blocks of brilliant, flat colors and abstract, angular shapes. Favorite motifs were simple, stylized flowers, fountains, leaping gazelles, sunbursts, and lightning zigzags. Ideas for these geometric patterns often came from Aztec and Egyptian art styles.

The influence of Aztec art can be seen in the geometric patterns on the coats worn by these Vogue *cover girls (1925).*

A TOTAL LOOK

All forms of the applied arts were affected by art deco, including textiles, graphics, and ceramics. Its greatest impact, however, was in the fields of architecture and interior design. Great temples to art deco include the Chrysler Building and Radio City Music Hall, both in New York City. Everything, from outside decoration to radiator grilles inside, was part of the look, and great attention was paid to the smallest detail.

A stylized art deco screen and tiled floor provide the perfect backdrop for this elegant outfit (1922).

LES BALLETS RUSSES

The arrival in Paris of the Russian Ballet, in 1909, is sometimes seen as the start of art deco. The Ballet's director, Sergei Diaghilev, used oriental-style costumes in vibrant colors — oranges, yellows, purples, jades, and pinks. This look reflected the gaiety of the early 1920s and was popularized by French designer Paul Poiret.

Costumes for the Ballets Russes' productions influenced fashion for many years. The costumes for Midnight Sun (*shown left and right*) *used rich embroidery and appliqué.*

Paul Poiret had been admired before the war for his exotic styles. In the 1920s, he led the way with minimalist, graphic styles of decoration.

TEXTILES AND PATTERNS

Two artists led the field of textiles: Russian-born Sonia Delaunay (1884–1979) and Frenchman Raoul Dufy (1877–1953). Both worked for the textile company Bianchini Férier, which specialized in hand-printed silks. Delaunay's designs often featured circles in bright colors. Dufy's textiles were bold, too; he would take a simple motif, such as a stylized turtle or vegetable, and copy it over and over for a great effect. Dufy worked with Paul Poiret (1879–1944) on fabrics for clothes and furnishings.

TONING IT DOWN

At first, art deco required lavish tambour embroidery, drawing inspiration from every possible source. By the mid-1920s, however, a less decorative look appeared. Detail was pared down to a few, carefully placed motifs. Fashionable interior designers favored white rooms with all-white furnishings, instead of color and patterns, and streamlined chrome and glass provided a modern feel.

In the early days of art deco (1923), decoration was as exotic as possible. Fashion plates were influenced by the East.

Vamps and Flappers

Having survived World War I, young people were determined to enjoy life to the fullest. Those from wealthy families were sometimes called "Bright Young Things." Their wild social lives centered around parties, nightclubs, and weekend house parties, and their fun-loving antics shocked the older generation.

Young women broke all the old rules by appearing in public without a chaperone.

FAST-LIVING GIRLS

Many young women adopted the new boyish look, danced all night, smoked in public, and wore makeup. They were called vamps or flappers. Women could now go out with friends without a chaperone. Nightclubs were the fashionable place to be seen, and cocktails became popular.

EYE-CATCHING EVENING WEAR

Evening dress was the same length as daywear. For impact, simple sheath dresses relied on fabulous fabrics and surface decoration, such as complicated beading.

For a night out on the town, an ostrich feather fan for cooling down was the most fashionable accessory. Another essential accessory was a long cigarette holder.

The flapper look was immortalized on the silver screen by Julie Andrews in the 1967 Hollywood film Thoroughly Modern Millie. Andrews plays a young girl who goes to New York in the 1920s.

Fancy dress balls, such as this one held in 1922, were all the rage. Many costumes, such as risqué belly-dancer outfits, had an eastern theme, some with exotic beading. Harlequin, or clown, suits were also favorites.

Another popular decoration was fringe, which provided movement. The emphasis was on the hips — drop-waisted dresses were trimmed with sashes or artificial flowers placed to one side along the waistline. Evening coats, made in rich brocades or velvets, fastened low on the hips and often had fur collars and cuffs.

SHEER STYLE

The nude look — bare arms, neck, and legs — was played up with the use of sheer fabrics, such as light silks, satins, chiffons, organzas, and tulles. Silver or gold lamé gave fashions an oriental or Arabian feel. Madeleine Vionnet became mistress of the "bias cut" — cutting fabric diagonally across the grain for a soft, draping effect. Dispensing with the corset, her shapes were fluid and simple. By the end of the decade, as skirt lengths dropped again, dresses were made with handkerchief points or uneven hems to look longer.

FINISHING TOUCHES

Long strings of beads or pearls suited the flat-fronted dresses, and earrings were worn long. The head was kept small and neat, and a band of fabric, perhaps with a feather in it, was stylish. Eyes were rimmed with makeup, and the eyelids were greased to make them shiny. Lips were painted bright red.

THE JAZZ AGE

The Dixieland Jazz Band, formed in New Orleans in 1916, started a craze for jazz and wild new dances! In 1926, the Charleston became popular. Performers such as American chorus girl Josephine Baker (1906–1975) were the height of fashion.

Dancing at the Folies-Bergère in Paris, Josephine Baker shocked the world with costumes made of a few ostrich feathers or beads — and little else!

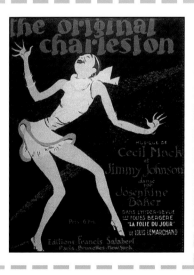

Madeleine Vionnet was known for the clever cut of her designs. The pointed hemline of this 1926 evening gown is emphasized by long silk tassels, front and back.

Sporty Styles

The new popularity of sports and outdoor activities meant the emphasis was now on a slim figure for both men and women. The clothing worn for these activities had a tremendous impact on fashion. Amelia Earhart (1898–1937), who flew solo across the Atlantic in 1932, even started her own fashion collection.

Skiwear in 1926: a waterproof skirt and jacket, with black-and-white calfskin trim.

FREEDOM TO MOVE

Many casual fashions of the 1920s and 1930s began as sportswear. Sporty clothes were lightweight and comfortable. The Norfolk suit, which was popular for boys and for everyday wear in the country, was originally worn for shooting. It had two deep pleats in the back of the jacket for ease of movement.

By 1934, sporty flannel trousers and tennis shorts featured state-of-the-art elastic waistbands.

TEE TIME TWEEDS

Golf was popular with both sexes. Men wore tweed or flannel plus-fours tucked into patterned socks. Women wore pleated, gored tweed skirts. Both sexes wore patterned sweaters or plain cardigans. Women also wore neck scarves and cloche hats.

ANYONE FOR TENNIS?

Sports stars became as glamorous and influenced fashion as much as film stars. Before French tennis star Suzanne Lenglen (1899–1938), women wore everyday clothes for tennis.

True plus-fours, worn for playing golf, hung 4 inches (10 centimeters) below the knee. Shorter plus-twos hung 2 inches (5 cm) below the knee.

Lenglen dressed in practical, short (calf-length), pleated tennis skirts and sleeveless dresses. She also appeared on the court without stockings, which was considered shocking. In 1933, Alice Marble (1913–1990) caused a sensation when she appeared at Wimbledon wearing shorts!

Lenglen's tennis wardrobe was created by French designer Jean Patou.

LE SKI

After women began competing in Olympic skiing in 1928, skiing became very popular. Elsa Schiaparelli (1890–1973) designed transparent oilskins and tortoiseshell goggles. Ski suits were made of waterproof gabardine, silk, wool, jersey, or corduroy. Cuffs fit tightly, thanks to the new Lastex yarn, and zippers made garments more practical.

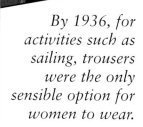

By 1936, for activities such as sailing, trousers were the only sensible option for women to wear.

SPORTS AND SHORTS

The fashion for slimness also promoted fitness activities. Women wore shorts for favorite pastimes, such as cycling and hiking, and they wore trousers for beach leisurewear.

SPORTY KNITS

Until the 1920s, knitwear was worn only as underwear or for sports. Polo sweaters were first worn by polo players and V-necks by cricketers. Sweaters were also worn by 19th-century health fanatics who exercised dressed in wool. From the early 1920s, bright, patterned sweaters were in vogue. Fair Isle knits became popular after the Duke of Windsor wore one on the golf course.

By the mid-1930s, knitwear designs were chic and monochrome.

Sun and Sand

Before the war, a suntan was a sign of being an outdoor laborer, but, in the 1920s, the rich and fashionable began to bare more skin at the beach. Sunbathing was considered healthful and was part of an increasing interest in outdoor activities.

Patou created these silk bathing shoes (1927) and the black-and-white bathing suit (right). Two-tone suits (left) were also in vogue.

Many more people had access to auto-mobiles, and jaunts to the seaside in a sporty, open-top car were very popular.

SUN WORSHIP

Resort areas, such as the French Riviera, Biarritz, and Le Touquet in France and California and Florida in the United States, became popular vacation destinations for the wealthy. Coco Chanel, one of the first of the fashionable to wear a tan, opened a boutique in Biarritz, in 1915, to cater to her rich clientèle. The middle and working classes also enjoyed seaside vacations, at camps such as Butlins.

Ocean liners were lavish, floating hotels. Cruises required a huge wardrobe, including full evening apparel for dinner dances and sunbathing outfits for lounging on the deck.

SKIMPY SWIMWEAR

Women's swimwear, which had previously looked like dresses with bloomers, got skimpier. The idea was to expose as much skin to the sun as possible. Bathing suits consisted of either a tunic-style top over long knickers, a one-piece costume, or, by the early 1930s, a daring two-piece — forerunner of the bikini. The suits were made from cotton, wool, or silk jersey fabric or were hand-knitted in wool. Because knitted suits tended to sag or shrink, manufacturers soon began to produce non-shrink, non-stretch yarn that kept its shape, and they supplied patterns to go with the yarn.

MACHO TRUNKS

Men, who had previously worn all-in-one bathing suits when ladies were present, began to wear topless trunks in the mid-1920s. Before this time, trunks had only been worn in competitions. They usually had a belt at the waist. Both men and women wore rubber bathing caps.

Stylish attire for the wealthy tourists in Biarritz included pleated wool and jersey skirts and cloche hats.

BEACH ACCESSORIES

Now that bathing suits were skimpier, more clothes were required for lounging on the beach. Terry cloth wraps and beach pajamas with wide legs were popular, as were halter-neck tops worn with shorts. Because people wanted a tan, painted parasols became less essential. People wore floppy straw or fabric hats to shade their eyes from the sun, until, during the 1930s, the hats came off and sunglasses became fashionable. To protect the feet, strappy sandals, espadrilles, or canvas shoes were fashionable.

This 1934 beach attire includes a straw hat, to shade eyes from the glaring sun, and strappy espadrilles, to protect feet from the burning sand.

SKIN CARE

In 1927, Jean Patou brought out the first suntan oil, called "Chaldee." Ambre Solaire was another early suncare product. Ordinary makeup also had to consider the new sun-kissed complexion. Max Factor introduced the color harmony approach and sold powders, lipsticks, and blusher that matched the wearer's skin tone.

By the 1930s, a wide range of suncare products was available, including a suntan oil called "Zon."

ZON SUN BATHING OIL
MAKES YOU A GLORIOUS BROWN

Prevents SUNBURN BLISTERING & IS ANTI-MIDGE BITE

1'6 & 2'9

The Great Depression

While a wealthy few enjoyed endless parties, most people were suffering the century's most serious economic crisis, the Great Depression. With high unemployment, trade unions and political movements struggled for more power.

In Great Britain, the General Strike of May 1926 caused total chaos.

Settlers traveled to the midwestern United States in search of a new life, but swirling dust storms destroyed their chances of finding it.

SOCIAL CONDITIONS

After the war, the gulf widened between the "haves" and the "have-nots." Housing conditions, health care, and education were poor. Although working-class communities were close-knit and supportive, many people were on breadlines. In 1926, workers in Great Britain called a General Strike in support of miners. The country came to a standstill for nine days. During the strike, some young socialites drove ambulances, buses, and streetcars, thinking it was fun. By the end of the 1920s, however, those same people had more sympathy for the workers.

In 1932, breadlines formed on Sixth Avenue and 42nd Street in New York City, as poor people lined up for handouts of free food.

In 1936, unemployed people, many nearly starving, marched on London from Jarrow, in northern England. These marchers made others aware of the unfairness in society.

STOCK MARKET CRASH

The 1929 Wall Street Crash caused a devastating economic depression, first in the United States and then all over Europe. Billions of dollars worth of shares were wiped out in less than a week of frantic selling on the New York Stock Exchange. Many speculators lost their life savings — some even committed suicide.

DUST TO DUST

During the 1930s, unemployment spiraled. As more workers were laid off, fewer people could afford to buy goods, so even more workers lost their jobs. In the United States, several years of drought, combined with over-farming in the Midwest, created a "Dustbowl" where nothing could grow. By digging up the prairies, farmers had lost the soil's natural protection from winds. People lost everything and moved back to the cities, but there was no work there, either.

It was an historic moment in 1937 when Italian leader Benito Mussolini visited German leader Adolf Hitler.

LA TRIBUNA ILLUSTRATA

LA STORICA VISITA DEL DUCE AL FÜHRER
I due Condottieri acclamati dal grande popolo tedesco

RIGHT-WING IDEAS ...

In Europe, extreme political movements emerged. Fascist leaders came to power, promising to restore national pride and create jobs. Benito Mussolini (1883–1945) took over in Italy in 1922. Austrian-born Adolf Hitler (1889–1945) came to power in Germany in 1933. Francisco Franco's (1892–1975) rule over Spain began in 1936.

WEALTHY EXCESSES

Germany was ripe for change when Hitler came to power. The Kit Kat Klub in Berlin, which was the setting of the 1972 film *Cabaret*, starring Liza Minelli, was a hotbed of vice and excess.

In the 1930s, most people in Germany were very poor, yet the rich indulged themselves.

... AND LEFT-WING IDEALS

Communism seemed to offer a solution. Its idea of shared work and shared wealth appealed to many people. The social concerns of the time affected fashion. Clothing became more sober in the 1930s, when people did not want their wealth to be conspicuous anymore.

Wit and Elegance

In the 1930s, the busy decoration of the previous decade gave way to a simple, streamlined look. The emphasis was on sophistication and elegance instead of boyish charm. Vamps and flappers grew up into modern women.

This long, fluid make-it-yourself dress was from a 1932 Vogue pattern book. The small clutch bag and elegant gloves pick up the black of the neckline and belted waist.

This fox fur coat by Schiaparelli is worn with a crushed-top hat (1938).

FEMININE FIGURES

By the late 1920s, hemlines had dropped, and waistlines had returned to their natural level. The shapeless *garçonne* look was replaced with a slim, curvy, feminine silhouette, and the decoration of the 1920s was replaced with clever seaming and stitching details. An increasing emphasis on shoulders looked forward to the wide, padded ones of the 1940s.

THE BIAS CUT

The greatest fashion innovation of the time was the bias cut, introduced by Parisian couturier, Madeleine Vionnet (1876–1975). Gores (flared panels, narrow near the waist and full at the hem) and flares were used instead of pleats. Dresses were made from printed silks, satins, georgettes, and crepe de chines, while smart day suits were made from jerseys and tweeds. Classic tailored suits could be made to measure or, more cheaply, bought ready-made. It was more important than ever to be slim — the new fashions did not allow for bulges. Women wore supple elastic girdles, and underwear, often bias-cut, had to be minimal and light.

Pattern books showed designs for simple but elegant clothes to make at home, such as these two stylish suits (1934).

Schiaparelli's hen hat (1938) added a touch of fun to a smart suit. Its brim is the bird's nest!

A plaid coat and a sealskin coat were in Schiaparelli's 1934 collection.

HATS

Hats were still stylish for daytime wear. They were small and neat, with a brim, and were often placed on the side of the head. The wittiest designs were created by Paris-based Elsa Schiaparelli. Her hats looked like broody chickens or lamb chops!

FOOT FIRST

At the beginning of the 1930s, shoes worn for daytime were sensible brogue lace-ups. Wedge heels and platforms were popular for casual and beach wear. Heels gradually became higher. Court shoes were stylish, too, but, with an increasing variety of footwear, sandals and slingbacks, high heels and low were all fashionable.

SCHIAPARELLI'S WILD STYLES

Elsa Schiaparelli was the most outrageous designer of the 1930s. She often worked with artists, including the surrealists Salvador Dali and Jean Cocteau, and was inventive down to the last detail. She made buttons shaped like circus acrobats, guitars, feathers, and lollipops. Her imagination ran wildest with accessories. One fantastic collaboration with Salvador Dali was the shoe hat (a hat that looks like an upside-down shoe).

These shoes by Schiaparelli are lavishly trimmed with fur.

Screen Idols

Movies became the most popular form of entertainment during the 1920s and 1930s. Film stars were idolized, as everyone tried to imitate the look and style of his or her favorite star.

VAMPS OF THE HAREM

The vamp look of the early 1920s was inspired by silent films — the term came from the vampire movies made at that time. The greatest vamp of all was Theda Bara (1890–1955). Her kohl-rimmed eyes, blood-red lips, and exotic outfits in *Cleopatra* (1917) and *Salomé* (1918) remained in vogue well into the 1920s. Gloria Swanson (1899–1983) was another sensuous star. She appeared in many films in the early 1920s before setting up her own film company.

FILMS AND FLAPPERS

American actresses Louise Brooks (1906–85) and Clara Bow (1905–65) were model flappers. Brooks' glossy bob still looks modern today, and Bow started a trend for painted, cupid's-bow lips.

Clara Bow became known as the "It" girl, after starring in the film It *(1927).*

Pin-ups of the age: the glamorous Gloria Swanson with actor Rudolph Valentino.

MOVIE MEN

The leading man of the 1920s was Italian-born Rudolph Valentino (1895–1926). Whether in an immaculate dinner suit or a sheikh's robes, he made women faint with admiration. His early death drove some fans to suicide. Cary Grant (1904–1986) always wore fine suits, while Fred Astaire's (1899–1987) outfits ranged from white tie and tails to open-necked shirts with slacks.

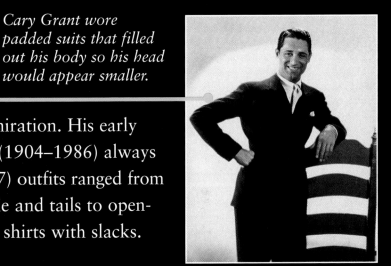

Cary Grant wore padded suits that filled out his body so his head would appear smaller.

GORGEOUS GARBO

Greta Garbo (1905–90) starred in twenty-seven films. Dressed by American designer Adrian (1903–59), she wore trousers, men's overcoats, and berets. For Garbo's role in *A Woman of Affairs* (1928), Adrian created a large, pull-down cloche, known as a slouch hat.

With minimal makeup and chic trouser suits, Greta Garbo popularized the masculine look.

COSTUMERS

Adrian also created bias-cut dresses for sex symbol Jean Harlow (1911–37) and for Joan Crawford (1904–86). Costumer Edith Head (1899–1981) created sultry clothes for Mae West (1882–1980) and for Marlene Dietrich (1901–1992). Although some fashion designers, including Coco Chanel, costumed movies, actual costumers understood the industry better and created looks that were not outdated by the time the film was released.

HOLLYWOOD HAIRSTYLES

Moviegoers avidly copied their idols. When Jean Harlow dyed her hair platinum blonde, many women copied her, even though the peroxide was painful and ruined their hair.

Even children braved the new permanent wave machines so they could have sleek curls.

Fred Astaire and Ginger Rogers wowed the world with their dance routines. From 1933 to 1949, they starred together in ten musicals.

Gangster Suits

London tailoring was still considered the best in the world. By the 1930s, however, the influence of Hollywood stars and well-dressed gangster celebrities had led the United States to set the style for men's fashions.

This 1936 lady's suit shows that pinstripes were not just for men.

ALL SORTS OF SUITS

Suits were made in lighter fabrics and louder patterns, such as checks and stripes. They were cut wide at the shoulders, gangster-style, and could be double- or single-breasted with wide, pointed lapels. Trousers were fastened with zippered flies instead of buttoned flies and were held up by a belt instead of suspenders.

A double-breasted overcoat (1927) gave a man a slim silhouette, especially when topped off with a banded trilby.

The single-breasted suit created a fuller look. Generously cut overcoats had wide shoulders and raglan sleeves to make them roomy and comfortable.

SUMMER STYLES

American style was most apparent in summer clothing and sportswear. Summer suits were made in fabrics such as crinkly seersucker, shantung (raw silk), and linen. Shorts and open-necked shirts were worn for leisure, and casual slacks, with zipped, blouson shirts or windbreakers, were worn for sport.

Sweaters became increasingly popular with suits or under a blazer with flannel trousers, but the patterned knitwear of the 1920s gave way to plainer designs in polo neck, cricket, and fishing styles. Footwear, too, was more lightweight and comfortable. Popular styles included suede shoes with crepe soles, loafers, canvas sneakers, and leather sandals.

HATS OFF FOR THE TRILBY

Hats were still popular for outdoor wear and always stylish for formal wear. The bowler and Homburg styles were worn to the office, while the favorite informal hat was the trilby with a silk band. Men wore a trilby with the brim snapped down at the front and up at the back. Hair that had been slicked back with brilliantine during the 1920s was now worn a little longer and softly waved.

TIMES THEY ARE A-CHANGIN'

Wristwatches were developed in the early part of the century so people could tell time easily when driving, traveling, or playing sports. They replaced pocket watches, which were still worn by the more old-fashioned men. During the 1930s, wristwatches were designed in stylish rectangular shapes that reflected the sleek modernism of the decade.

Gangster Al Capone (center) was arrested in 1931.

GANGSTERS

During Prohibition in the United States (1920–1933), gangs controlled the sale of illegal alcohol on the black market. In the St. Valentine's Day Massacre (1929), Al Capone's gang shot seven men from a rival Chicago gang.

The Public Enemy (1931), *starring James Cagney, popularized the gangster look.*

Front to Back

In the 1930s, women's evening wear became very sophisticated. Full-length evening gowns that plunged at the back were the most tantalizing style of the decade.

Actress Joan Barry wore this backless gown in The Port *(1933). The full, flared sleeves and the bow at the back emphasized her bare skin.*

Molyneux's yellow gown (1936) had a skirt that separated to show a flash of leg as the wearer walked. In another Molyneux design, a generous scarf drapes low to show off the back and the nape of the neck.

BACK OFF

Evening gowns were typically high at the front and cut down to the waist at the back. The back of the dress was also the focal point for such detailing as drapes, bows, and accessories. American designer Mainbocher (1891–1976) used the bias cut very effectively in his gowns, and he designed short, bolero jackets to wear over the top. He was the favorite designer of Wallis Warfield Simpson and created the dress she wore when she married the Duke of Windsor.

SLINKY AND SEXY

The bias cut produced a hip-hugging silhouette that flared out toward the ankles. Slippery satins, fluid crepes, sheer voiles, and slinky silks, in solid colors or floral prints, emphasized this slim, streamlined look. These fabrics were sometimes embroidered or overlaid with lace to create styles that harked back to the romantic past.

This lamé creation by Lelong (1934) revisits the turn-of-the-century bustle. The dress features a hooded cape, called a capuchon, which drapes over the back in folds.

Other features borrowed from the past included bustles, which showed off the tightness of the dress on the hip; short trains; and elegant fantails, as designed by Schiaparelli.

CHEAPER CLOTH

Although the fuller lines of garments required more fabric than in the 1920s, a response to the economic depression could be seen in the use of cheaper fabrics for evening wear. In 1931, Chanel's collection included thirty-five evening gowns in different types of cotton — piqué, lace, muslin, organdy, lawn, and net. At the bottom end of the market, artificial silk, or rayon, was used.

FURS

Wearing fur was very popular throughout the 1920s and 1930s. All kinds of furs were used, including monkey, leopard, and ocelot. Fox fur was especially fashionable; one or two skins, held together by clips in the foxes' mouths, were worn around the shoulders. Women did not consider where the furs came from — they were just another expression of glamour.

The extravagant ermine evening coat had a fox fur collar.

DIAMONDS FOREVER

As in the 1920s, long strands of beads were fashionable, but now they were worn slung over the back. Small studs and clips replaced long dangly earrings. Chunky jewelry in geometric shapes showed the influence of art deco. Some of Cartier's designs, at this time, teamed diamonds with other precious stones, such as sapphires or emeralds, to create fantastical jewelry in the shapes of animals. With the economic depression, however, it was considered bad taste to display wealth, and accessories were generally kept simple.

A slim evening gown by Schiaparelli (1934) shows her trademark wit. A stiff fantail highlights the narrow hips above. A shiny, patterned jacket completes the design.

In May 1938, embroidery and floral prints harked back to the tea gowns worn thirty years earlier. Now, however, these floor-sweeping styles were only for evening wear.

The Technology of Fashion

The 1920s and 1930s saw many new developments in the textile industry. The first artificial fabric, rayon, was developed and used extensively. This period also saw the production of new elastic yarns and important advances in knitting.

THE BIRTH OF RAYON

Rayon is an artificial fiber because it is not found in nature. Although manufactured by human beings, it is not a synthetic because it is made from natural materials — wood pulp or wood chips. The process for making rayon was discovered in 1892, ending a long search that started in the 1600s. The first artificial silk plant opened in the United States in 1910, and, in 1924, the new yarn was named *rayon*.

THE RAYON YEARS

Rayon's low cost made it a popular fabric for those who could not afford real silk. In 1920, when hemlines rose, women wanted to wear "silk" stockings, giving the hosiery industry a huge boost. By the end of the 1930s, however, nylon stockings replaced rayon ones.

Rayon's silky feel made it ideal for the slinky gowns of the 1930s, such as this one in white, satiny rayon (1936).

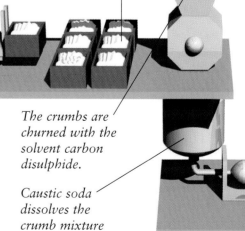

Sheets of cellulose made from wood pulp are soaked in caustic soda.

The sheets are broken into fluffy flakes called cellulose crumbs.

The crumbs are aged for up to three days.

The crumbs are churned with the solvent carbon disulphide.

Caustic soda dissolves the crumb mixture to make viscose.

in the 1920s and 1930s

NATTY KNITS

The 1920s saw a huge expansion of the knitting industry as knitwear became fashionable for outer garments instead of just for underwear and sportswear. Industrial knitting machines could produce enormous quantities of either flat or circular jersey material that could be cut into shapes and sewn together afterward, or fully fashioned garments that were shaped by the machine.

This short-sleeved sweater from the mid-1930s shows how advances in knitting allowed for elaborate designs with contrasting ribbed panels.

Textile workers operated power knitting looms in Minneapolis in 1936.

FANTASTIC ELASTIC

Another important development of the 1920s and 1930s was the creation of elastic yarns. Improved methods of collecting natural rubber resulted in longer strands that could be made into yarn. In 1931, Lastex, which had a core of rubber with cotton, silk, wool, or rayon around it, appeared on the market, spelling the beginning of a whole new era of stretchier, more comfortable clothes.

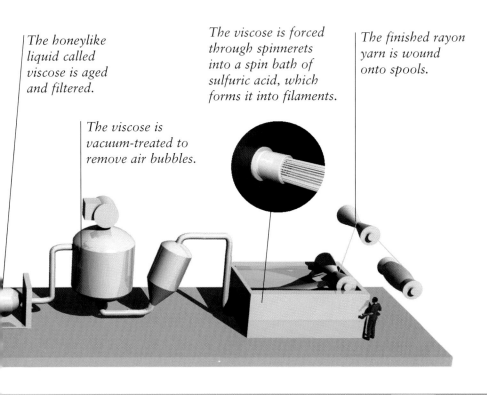

The honeylike liquid called viscose is aged and filtered.

The viscose is vacuum-treated to remove air bubbles.

The viscose is forced through spinnerets into a spin bath of sulfuric acid, which forms it into filaments.

The finished rayon yarn is wound onto spools.

Elastic waistbands held up trousers without the need for suspenders.

· T I M E L I N E ·

	FASHION	WORLD EVENTS	TECHNOLOGY	FAMOUS PEOPLE	ART & MEDIA
1920	•First elasticized bathing suit, by Jantzen	•U.S. women get vote •Prohibition (to 1933)	•First hairdryer	•Joan of Arc canonized	•D. H. Lawrence: Women in Love
1921	•Chanel No. 5 perfume launched	•Chinese communist party founded	•Insulin discovered	•Marie Stopes opens Britain's first birth control clinic	•Valentino stars in The Sheik
1922	•Duke of Windsor starts Fair Isle trend	•Russia becomes USSR	•Choc-ice (Eskimo pies)	•Tutankhamen's tomb opened •Gandhi jailed (to 1924)	•James Joyce: Ulysses •T. S. Eliot: The Wasteland
1923	•Edith Head begins work in Hollywood	•Italy: Mussolini seizes power	•Autogiro (early helicopter) flown in Spain		•Cecil B. de Mille: The Ten Commandments
1924	•Patou puts monogram on his clothing	•Britain: first Labour government elected	•First superhighway opens, in Italy	•Lenin dies	•Gershwin: Rhapsody in Blue
1925	•Adrian begins work in Hollywood		•Scotch tape	•George Bernard Shaw wins Nobel Prize for Literature	•F. Scott Fitzgerald: The Great Gatsby
1926		•Britain: General Strike •Mussolini's dictatorship	•J. L. Baird: first television •Godard: first rocket	•Ederle swims the English Channel •Valentino dies	•Fritz Lang: Metropolis
1927	•Patou brings out first suntan oil	•German stock market collapses	•First Volvo car •Polyesters first used	•Charles Lindbergh: first solo flight across Atlantic	•First successful "talkie": The Jazz Singer
1928		•USSR: Stalin's first five-year plan	•Discovery of penicillin •Electric razor patented	•Emeline Pankhurst dies	•Walt Disney: First Mickey Mouse cartoon
1929	•Schiaparelli's first full collection	•USA: Wall Street Crash		•U.S.: Hoover elected president	•Mondrian: Composition in a Square
1930	•Mainbocher opens salon in Paris	•India: Gandhi leads Salt March protest	•Planet Pluto identified	•Amy Johnson: first woman to fly to Australia	•Chrysler Building completed •Dietrich in The Blue Angel
1931		•Japanese army occupies Chinese Manchuria	•Lastex yarn introduced	•Al Capone arrested for tax fraud	•Dali: Limp Watches •Cagney in The Public Enemy
1932		•Nazis take control of Reichstag (parliament)	•Polyethylene created •First radio telescope	•Amelia Earhart flies solo across Atlantic	•Carwardine creates "Anglepoise" lamp
1933	•Alice Marble wears shorts at Wimbledon	•Hitler in power as Chancellor of Germany	•Lemaître proposes Big Bang theory		•Fay Wray in King Kong •Garbo in Queen Christina
1934	•Lelong launches ready-to-wear "editions"	•China: Communists led by Mao on Long March	•Nylon •Cat's-eye road studs first used	•Shirley Temple wins an Oscar at age six	
1935	•Schiaparelli uses zipper as a design statement	•Italy invades Abyssinia (Ethiopia)	•Germany: First TV broadcasting station built	•Malcolm Campbell sets 300 mph land speed record	•Astaire and Rogers in Top Hat
1936		•Spanish Civil War begins •Edward VIII abdicates	•Volkswagen Beetle designed by Porsche	•Jessie Owens stars at Berlin Olympics	•Frank Lloyd Wright: Falling Water
1937		•India: Congress Party wins elections	•Ballpoint pen •Polyurethanes discovered		•Picasso: Guernica •Walt Disney: Snow White
1938	•Polaroid sunglasses invented	•Germany and Austria unite (Anschluss)	•Teflon discovered		
1939	•Schiaparelli: first perfume for men ("Snuff")	•Spanish Civil War ends •World War II begins	•Heinkel built first jet aircraft	•Sigmund Freud dies	•Selznick: Gone With the Wind •Garland in The Wizard of Oz

Glossary

art deco: a design style that featured angular shapes and brilliant colors.

art nouveau: a design style that featured plant and flower forms with graceful, curving lines.

bias cut: a way of cutting fabric diagonally to make it fall into clinging folds.

bustle: a pad or framework that supported the fullness of fabric at the back of a skirt.

communism: a political and social system that promotes shared work and shared wealth, abolishing private property in favor of collective ownership.

crepe de chine: thin, subtly-wrinkled cloth made of silk or rayon.

cubism: a modern art style that featured abstract, geometric shapes and fragmented forms.

Depression: a period marked by a severe slump in economic activity and a sharp rise in unemployment.

fascism: a dictatorial political system that enforces state control of all aspects of society.

frock coat: an almost knee-length, usually double-breasted man's coat.

futurism: a modern art style that gave expression to energy, movement, speed, and mechanical processes.

lamé: a shiny fabric made by interweaving metallic threads with silk, wool, or other fibers.

Lastex: the trade name for an elastic yarn consisting of a rubber core coated with silk, cotton, wool, or rayon.

plus-fours: baggy trousers, similar to knickers, that ended 4 inches (10 cm) below the knee.

spat: a cloth or leather shoe covering over the ankle and the instep, usually fastened under the instep with a strap.

tambour: embroidery done on a tambour frame that stretched fabric tightly between two hoops.

More Books to Read

The 1920s. The 1930s. Fashion Sourcebooks (series). John Peacock (Thames and Hudson)

Chanel Fashion Review: Paper Dolls in Color. Tom Tierney (Dover)

Everyday Fashions of the Thirties As Pictured in Sears Catalogs. Stella Blum, editor (Dover)

Fashion Designer. Fashion World (series). Miriam Moss (Crestwood House)

Fashion Through the Ages: From Overcoats to Petticoats. Margaret Knight and Penny Ives (Viking Press)

Fashions of a Decade: The 1920s. Jacqueline Herald (Facts on File)

Fashions of the Thirties: 476 Authentic Copyright-Free Illustrations. Dover Pictorial Archive (series). Carol Belanger Grafton (Dover)

Schiaparelli Fashion Review: Paper Dolls in Full Color. Tom Tierney (Dover)

Where Will This Shoe Take You?: A Walk Through the History of Footwear. Laurie Lawlor (Walker & Co. Library)

Web Sites

Flapper Culture and Style: Louise Brooks and the Jazz Age. *www.pandorasbox.com/flapper.html*

Just Jewelry Searches for Schiaparelli! *www.jstjewelry.com/searchingfor.htm*

Timeline of Costume History.
20th Century Western Costume: 1920-1930 *www.costumes.org/pages/timelinepages/1920s1.htm*
20th Century Western Costume: 1930-1940 *www.costumes.org/pages/timelinepages/1930s1.htm*

Due to the dynamic nature of the Internet, some web sites stay current longer than others. To find additional web sites, use a reliable search engine with one or more of the following keywords: *art deco, Louise Brooks, Chanel, clothing, costumes, fabric, fashion, flappers, gangsters, hats, Edith Head, jazz age, rayon, Schiaparelli, shoes, tweed,* and *Vionnet.*

Index